KEEP IT
SIMPLE

KEEP IT
SIMPLE

A guide to a happy, relaxed home.

Atlanta Bartlett & Dave Coote
Photography by Polly Wreford

RYLAND PETERS & SMALL
LONDON • NEW YORK

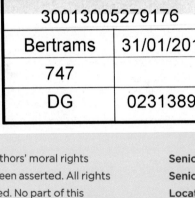
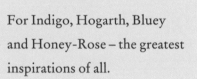

For Indigo, Hogarth, Bluey and Honey-Rose – the greatest inspirations of all.

First published in 2015
by Ryland Peters & Small
20–21 Jockey's Fields,
London WC1R 4BW
and
341 East 116th Street,
New York NY 10029

www.rylandpeters.com

10 9 8 7 6 5 4 3 2

Text © Atlanta Bartlett
and Dave Coote 2015
Design and photographs ©
Ryland Peters & Small 2015

ISBN: 978-1-84975-621-1

Printed and bound in China

Senior Designer Megan Smith
Senior Commissioning Editor Annabel Morgan
Location Research Jess Walton
Head of Production Patricia Harrington
Art Director Leslie Harrington
Editorial Director Julia Charles
Publisher Cindy Richards

CONTENTS

OUR INSPIRATION **6**   HOW IT WORKS **10**

THE SIMPLE MINDSET

DITCH FASHION **14**   DECLUTTER **22**   SAVE MONEY…& THE PLANET **28**
BE IN TOUCH WITH NATURE **36**   RELAX & ENJOY YOURSELF **44**

MAKING IT HAPPEN

THE BONES **56**   COLOUR **70**   FURNITURE **88**   FABRICS **102**
DETAILS & ACCESSORIES **110**

LIVING THE DREAM

SITTING ROOMS & COSY NOOKS **126**   COOKING & EATING **134**   SLEEPING &
WASHING **144**   WORK SPACES **154**   ONE-SPACE LIVING **158**   THE OUTDOORS **162**

PICTURE CREDITS **170**   SOURCES **172**   INDEX **174**   ACKNOWLEDGMENTS **176**

OUR INSPIRATION

We are all visual creatures, steeped in personal visual references that we absorb every day and store away in the depths of our subconscious. Both of us were born in London and we share many mental images that stem from growing up in that vibrant, eclectic city during the 1970s and early '80s. Gritty subcultures like punk, rockabilly and soul were as much a part of our educations as more formal cultural experiences such as visits to the Wallace Collection, an afternoon at the V&A or a walk around the Tate Gallery. But it doesn't stop there. Inspiration is a never-ending journey of exploration and discovery, and it comes in many shapes and forms – poems, films, walks on the beach, postcards, holidays, books, history, a chair leg or a scrap of fabric are all part of the process too. The current social climate and our changing planet also have a part to play. In our fast-paced, consumer-driven lives, set against a backdrop of worldwide economic problems, we see a need for a more realistic and responsible attitude to design. Houses that have been designed as status symbols, or the notion of design for design's sake, have never appealed. We prefer a holistic approach and believe a home should, first and foremost, be a place for living. We also draw inspiration from practical considerations and the simple things in life, such as spending quality time with our family and minimizing our carbon footprint through use of sustainable materials, recycling and repairing wherever possible.

There are so many visual references filed away in our minds that it would be impossible to list them all and it amazes us that we always manage to recall exactly the right one when seeking inspiration for a particular project. But for us, the biggest influence of all is each other, as our differences send us off in new directions. Yin and yang, rough with smooth, feminine and masculine, utility with glamour, nature versus man-made. These are the building blocks of our design philosophy and partnership.

HOW IT WORKS

Keep it Simple is not a book about a decorating style but a way of life. Yes, style is important, but creating a relaxed and happy home encompasses so much more than just the look of a place. It involves rediscovering what's really important in life through self-expression, rejecting materialism, appreciating simple pleasures, accepting the imperfect and making a home that you and your family can really enjoy living in.

To begin, in The Simple Mindset we explore the early stages of the design process and encourage you to think long and hard about what home means to you and how you like to live. Change is a real and inescapable part of family life, but when it comes to interior design, change can be an expensive business, so it is vital that you get the structural elements right from the start, allowing you to play around with the details as you and your family grow and change. This may be a daunting prospect for the inexperienced decorator, so in Making it Happen we explain how to navigate the practicalities, from building issues right through to the finishing touches. Finally, in Living the Dream, we investigate the home room by room and provide a multitude of ideas and suggestions to help you put together an interior that is right for you.

We wanted to create a book that is really useful so we have broken down all these elements into easily digestible nuggets of information that you can dip in and out of, depending on your mood or the current state of your home or project. We hope that you find it helpful, informative and inspirational.

THE SIMPLE MINDSET

Five steps to living a simple life.

DITCH FASHION

Trusting in your individuality and allowing your own style to shine through is the first step towards making a happy and relaxed home. The fashion world can be an invaluable source of inspiration, but its dictatorial nature can block personal creativity. The key is to acknowledge what's in fashion now, take what you like from it and ditch the rest. It is very easy to be seduced by current trends, but the very nature of fashion demands a certain level of consumerism that jars with our Simple Mindset; after all, anyone can follow fashion if they spend enough money. Don't be daunted – just follow our three golden bywords. Function: many of the best designs spring from utility and a room that fulfils its intended purpose will always have a deep-rooted integrity. Longevity: the addition of classic, well-made pieces will always ensure a timeless elegance and save you money in the long run. Self-expression: your home is your sanctuary, so adorn it with things you love and that make you happy to ensure a nurturing and cosseting environment. A more personal, organic style of decorating that transcends fashion will be the result.

FIND YOUR STYLE

It can be difficult to hold on to our individuality when magazines, TV makeover shows and chain stores bombard us with advice on what to wear and how to decorate. But an interior lifted from the pages of a glossy magazine will always have a slightly soulless quality. We believe a home should be a true reflection of its inhabitants, their tastes and their way of life, and as long as you follow a few easy rules and get the bare bones of your interior in place first (more on this later), any amount of self-expression will hang together.

Start off with some self-analysis: what works for you and how do you like to live? Do you like a laid-back vibe or prefer a more ordered, formal feel? Are you drawn to light, fresh colours or are you happiest

enveloped in richer, darker shades? This sort of questioning will really help you identify your own style. It's also important to make educated choices, so become familiar with different fabrics and materials, how they drape and what their limitations are. Research and gather information about historical interiors or other cultures. Once you have a grasp of these things, you will be better placed to play with different styles and develop your own. Above all, don't be afraid to experiment – trial and error is the best way to discover your own style, as we learn as much from our mistakes as we do from our successes.

In a surprising mix of elements, elegant classical furniture contrasts with rustic, wood-clad walls to create an individual yet cohesive look (left). Rich, dark brown vintage leather armchairs blend perfectly with the original woodwork of a salvaged Victorian railway carriage/railroad car that has been cleverly converted into a home by the sea (above). The natural theme pulls together a slightly incongruous mix of items in our wooden beach house, while the vibrant 1970s light helps to add an unexpected twist (opposite).

A strong beach theme – pebbles, coral, bare boards – helps to create an ethereal and light-hearted feel in this gorgeous cabin.

TELL A STORY

Our emotional response to where we live is paramount. While your home should reflect your lifestyle, interests and passions, it should also be somewhere that soothes your emotions; a place where you can relax, recharge your batteries and be inspired. Designers and advertisers have long been aware of the power of storytelling in creating a collection or selling a product, and the same concept can be applied to your home. When it comes to decorating a space, creating a visual narrative is a powerful tool.

For instance, an easy-going, beach-chic theme could bring a carefree, holiday mood to an interior, while a book-lined library might be conducive to study. Of course, these are generalizations and everyone has different emotional responses, but the idea is to think about how you would like to feel when in a particular space and then to go about creating that mood by telling a visual story. A word of warning, though – none of us wants to live on a stage set, so once you have the foundations of your story in place, throw the look off course by adding a few unexpected twists so the finished space is a personal retreat, not a theme park.

Decorative elements are important when telling a visual story. A galvanized metal tray plays host to lime green hydrangeas, a starfish and sea dollars in a narrative of honest, natural materials (above left). Wood planking, a rolltop tub and a chandelier create a romantic, rustic mood in this cabin (above centre). Colour and texture can be used to great effect to keep a theme going, as this collection of corals and decorative plasterwork illustrates (above right).

BELIEVE IN YOURSELF

True style comes from within. It is born of bravery and self-conviction, so trust your own taste and don't be afraid to combine styles that might not be considered as 'going together'. If you want to team ethnic kilims with blowzy chintz curtains, go for it. If you love French country style and the industrial factory look, mix the two. Can't decide if you're a maximalist or a minimalist? Do both! It's the combination of elements that determines our individual styles and ultimately makes a house a home. Remember, perfection is not the aim. Style is not about looking as if you live in a show home – it's about showing that you know how to enjoy every part of your life at home.

DECLUTTER

Most of us have far too much stuff. While we dream of living the simple life with possessions kept to the bare minimum, in reality few of us are that disciplined. Decluttering your home is an essential part of the Keep it Simple way, as it helps you focus on what really matters in life – less stuff equals less to clean, less debt, less stress and less to organize, not to mention a more aesthetically pleasing home.

Although each of us has a different tolerance threshold to clutter, we should all be able to pare down our possessions to some extent. Start small. Give yourself five minutes each day to clear a surface or to tidy a cupboard one shelf at a time. Have some fun and set your family the 10-10-10 challenge – each of you must find 10 items to throw away, 10 to donate and 10 to put away in their proper home. A family of four could rack up an amazing 120 items in a short space of time!

For a wardrobe bursting at the seams, try the coat hanger experiment – turn every hanger in your closet the wrong way round, then as you wear each item, replace it with the hanger the right way round. After a while, you will see exactly which items you wear and which items you can live without.

ORGANIZE

A well-organized home will be a smooth-running one, so get your head in gear and take a long, hard look at your possessions. Be ruthless – get rid of anything that you do not love, need, or use regularly. Think carefully about how you live and arrange your house accordingly, storing like with like so that items can be easily found when they are needed and just as easily put away again when you have finished with them.

Once you have decided that something is worth keeping, give it a proper home. Antique apothecary chests are an attractive and practical way to store all those small miscellaneous items such as pens, phone chargers, sunglasses, keys and batteries, while the family shoe problem can be solved by a set of old

school-gym cubbyholes positioned as close as possible to the front door. If you can't track one down, look out for vintage office storage instead, or fashion your own storage out of fruit crates stacked on their sides.

In the kitchen, make sure that unloading the dishwasher is a quick and easy task by storing everyday items within an arm's length of the machine, while in the laundry room or linen cupboard, storing bed linen sets together inside one pillowcase will ensure that you can always find exactly what you need without pulling the whole cupboard out each time.

Multitasking cubbyholes have been built into the structure of this converted railway carriage/railroad car by the sea, providing some much-needed storage, while also creating an attractive focal point (opposite). If you can afford the space, a scullery leading off the main kitchen is a great place to store any infrequently used kitchen items (left). An antique plan chest offers plenty of space to keep all those small items to hand in an organized manner (above).

In this beachside cabin, a wall of cupboards with doors made from reclaimed shutters houses a tiny en-suite bathroom as well as storage for bed linen, clothes and shoes (far left). A high shelf over the oven in our kitchen supports a collection of white china and bridges the gap between storage and display (left). Taking the time to make the inside of a cupboard beautiful will bring some joy to everyday tasks. In this mint green cabinet, the shelves have been lined with toile-de-jouy wallpaper (below).

STORAGE

Plenty of storage is the secret to every successfully designed interior. You can lavish money and attention on the décor of your home, but if it doesn't work on a practical level, it's a failure. Good storage is crucial and needs to be factored in at the early stages of the design process so that a certain amount can be incorporated into the structure of the rooms.

One storage solution is to donate an entire wall to a row of built-in cupboards. You will, of course, lose some of the footprint of the room, but what you lose in centimetres/inches you gain in storage space, which in the end will make the room feel bigger. You could conceal the cupboards behind clever panelling or make a feature of them by using antique shutters or vintage mirrors as doors.

Freestanding storage is also invaluable; perhaps an antique linen press in the kitchen or a pastel-coloured 1950s kitchen cupboard with a pull-down work surface to hold home office paraphernalia. Don't make the mistake of thinking that everything has to be hidden away. Everyday items such as plates and glasses in the kitchen or jewellery in the bedroom make great decorative displays, with the benefit of being close to hand when needed.

In our studios near the south coast of England, the double-height ceilings means that everything has to be scaled up to look in proportion. This huge armoire with a pair of tall, antique fretwork doors from the South of France takes centre stage, while a narrow dining table has been reinvented as a console table with the addition of industrial castors to raise its height.

SAVE MONEY...
& THE PLANET

We live in a material world and it's no secret that our fast-paced consumerism and disposable attitude to throw-away trends is proving a huge drain on the planet. But there is a revolution brewing and our grandparents' habit of patching up and letting nothing go to waste has been adopted by forward-thinking designers.

Far from being a passing fad, recycling, upcycling, retro-fitting or whatever you want to call it is here to stay, and rightly so. The need to save energy, preserve natural resources and protect the planet plays a vital role in the design world, and it's important not to brand this stance as a style statement but to see it as a way of life. We can all play our part by checking our constant desire for 'new' things. Starting to accept the imperfect and embracing the idea of repair and reuse will encourage an ethically responsible approach to decorating our homes.

What is really exciting for us is that the new wave of creativity inspired by greener living is paving the way for innovative ideas that are both easy on the eye and on your conscience. A clever recycler might be so subtle about using another person's junk that the finished piece will show no signs of its second-hand nature. And there is also much credit to be had in celebrating the heritage and history of an item so that its past life and purpose remains an integral part of its new-found beauty.

RECYCLE

Recycling is at the heart of our Simple Mindset philosophy, as it forces us to shun the easy option of chain-store shopping and get creative, offers an opportunity to offset our carbon footprints and also helps us develop an individual sense of style. Think carefully about what you rip out when refurbishing a house and save anything that can be reused. Stained boards might make new cupboard doors, for instance, while old copper piping can be refashioned into curtain poles. Use old doors to panel a wall or combine bricks and ceiling joists to create a coffee table. Second-hand furniture is inexpensive and ethically sound, and it's often the old paintwork or patina that lends a piece its charm, but if not, give it a new lease of life with a lick of eco-friendly paint.

In our busy family kitchen, different types of recyclable materials are sorted into various vintage enamel pails (above). These cabinet doors were made from wood saved from a ceiling that was torn down in another part of the building during renovation work (opposite and above right). The vintage wooden sink surround and draining board comprises two separate work surfaces that have been spliced together to fit the space, with no attempt made to hide or fill the holes left by the original taps/faucets. Scaffolding planks were painted and used to make the shelving above, while ex-army billycans hold the cutlery.

Uncovered at the back of a junk shop, this elegant metal table started life as a vice/vise-stand. The vice was removed and found a new role in Dave's workshop, liberating the base for reinvention as a pretty piece of furniture that belies its workhorse origins.

A vintage metal bird cage makes a charming hanging light. The vibrant pink cord and the squirrel-cage bulb lend it a modern edge (far left). Usually concealed behind panelling, this copper pipework has become the main feature of these custom-made taps/faucets (left). Tin hot and cold signs hang from simple pieces of twisted wire to ensure that no one gets scalded. Another great upcycling idea is this glass pendant light created from an old French spirit bottle (below).

RE-THINK

The process of repurposing a useless or unwanted item into something new and useful, otherwise known as upcycling, is the perfect way to save money and the planet. Student design shows are awash with inspiring upcycling ideas, such as armchairs made from old bathtubs and chests of drawers made from plastic bottles, but do you really want to live with these? Of course, extreme ideas are what start revolutions and they certainly have their value, but the beauty is that we can take those concepts and adapt them to suit our own lives.

The possibilities are endless if you think outside the box. Vintage headscarves or worn-out sweaters can be fashioned into cushion covers, industrial metal funnels repurposed as light shades and old tin cans as tea light holders once you have hammered a few holes in them. Before you throw away that unwanted chest of drawers, think about adding castors to the bottom of the drawers to create roll-away under-bed storage, or salvage the wood from old pallets to panel a wall. In the bathroom, an old mangle table could make a quirky sink stand (you will need to cut a hole in the enamel top), while old grain sacks make the perfect bathmat.

MAKE DO AND MEND

The quest to be kind on our pockets and lighten the load on the environment by cutting back on consumerism, learning to appreciate the imperfect and working with what you have is a huge part of the Simple Mindset. Although originally launched in 1941 as part of the war effort, the idea of 'Make do and Mend' has as much relevance today as it did back then. In a backlash against our throw-away society, repair is becoming cool again and the Repair Cafés popping up in every neighbourhood serve to prove the point. Giving something a new lease of life by mending it is very satisfying and we should all be re-educating ourselves in the arts of fixing, darning and patching. Dutch website Platform 21's Repair Manifesto says 'every time we repair something we add to its history, its soul and its inherent beauty', as anyone who has ever bought an antique linen sheet and come across a beautifully stitched patch where the previous owner has painstakingly mended a hole can confirm.

A wall panel covered with vintage wallpaper has been reinvented as a bedhead (above left). Making do is sometimes preferable to mending: the crumbling plaster and exposed pipework in this 16th-century farmhouse have a character and charm that it would be a crime to 'fix' (above right). A meticulously stitched patch from years ago only adds to this cushion's appeal (opposite above left). Even though some drawers are missing from this antique plan chest, it is still functional and beautiful (opposite above right).

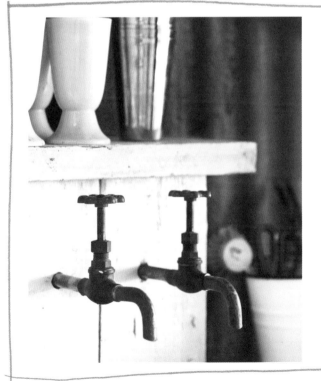

Refit and reuse

As the saying goes, necessity is the mother of invention. Thomas Edison declared 'To invent, you need a good imagination and a pile of junk', and embarking on a project with the criteria of saving money and conserving resources can be an inspiring starting point. Kitchen and bathroom taps/faucets are one of the heftier investments that you will have to make when decorating your home. Antique and vintage models are beautiful and might seem like a good alternative to their modern-day counterparts, but unless they have been fully reconditioned (which adds considerably to their price tag), they are not likely to work very well. As an alternative, why not ask a friendly plumber to custom-make taps/faucets using copper piping and a couple of stopcocks, as we have done here. Simple, functional and easy to repair, they have a utilitarian beauty all of their own.

BE IN TOUCH WITH NATURE

Nature grounds us. An appreciation for and love of the natural world is an integral part of the human psyche, and scientists have proved that being surrounded by nature improves our healing and cognitive abilities and reduces stress levels and aggression – a walk along a leafy path is said to lift our energy levels far more effectively than that cup of coffee we tend to reach for. No wonder then that striving to be in touch with nature is another important step towards creating a happy and relaxed home.

Cooking and eating alfresco always bring about a sense of wellbeing, and if you are lucky enough to have an outside space, then make the most of it and transform your garden into an extension of your interior. Install a fire pit that you can cook on and sit around in comfy chairs and sofas, hang glass jars containing tea lights from the trees and create for yourself an outside retreat that is just as welcoming as any cosy sitting room.

Gardening is another great way to de-stress, so get outside and start digging. If you don't have a garden, then a herb box on your windowsill will have a similar effect, as will small touches like a bowl of pebbles collected on the beach or a simple bunch of flowers on the kitchen table.

BLURRING THE BOUNDARIES

Bringing the outside in is a great way to be in touch with nature all year round. Glass sliding doors are the obvious choice when trying to make the garden or terrace seem as if it is part of your interior, but bi-folding or French doors will also do the trick. The idea is to make the transition from inside to outside as imperceptible as possible, so incorporating nature into your home in the form of materials such as timber panelling, bare wood floors, slubby fabrics and raw textures will all help to blur the boundaries. The colour scheme can also help enhance a natural theme, with pale neutrals and blues evoking a seaside feel, for example, while darker, earthier colours might conjure up images of a cabin in the woods.

Rough-cut logs cover the walls in this cabin at the bottom of our garden (left). Self-seeded cow parsley grows all the way up to the back door of this railway carriage/railroad car home, making the threshold between inside and out almost seamless (opposite).

GROW YOUR OWN

Fig chutney – quick, easy and delicious!

INGREDIENTS

2 small cinnamon sticks; 2 tablespoons whole cloves; 1.5 kg/3¼ lb. fresh figs, chopped; 3 large onions, finely chopped; 3 cloves of garlic, crushed; 2 teaspoons ground allspice; 2 teaspoons ground ginger; 2 tablespoons salt; 450 g/2¼ cups soft light brown sugar; 450 g/ 2¼ cups Demerara/raw sugar; 1.2 litres/5 cups malt vinegar.

Parcel up the cinnamon sticks and cloves in a piece of muslin/ cheesecloth and tie with cook's string/twine. Place all the ingredients including the muslin/cheesecloth parcel into a large preserving pan. Bring to the boil, turn down the heat and simmer for 2–3 hours, stirring occasionally, until almost all the vinegar has evaporated and your wooden spoon leaves a channel for a few seconds after dragging it across the bottom of the pan. Spoon the chutney into warm sterilized jars and seal. It tastes best after being allowed to mature for 2–3 months, although we never seem to be able to leave it that long!

Gardening is a great leveller. On a different timescale to the rest of our busy lives, it gets us outside, puts us in touch with nature and is something the whole family can join in with. There is nothing more satisfying than eating something that you have grown yourself or picking home-grown flowers for the hallway. However small your plot, we urge you to give it a go, even if it is only a pot of tomatoes on a balcony four storeys up.

If you have the space for a vegetable patch and cutting garden, raised beds are a boon, as they make it easier to maintain soil quality and are far kinder on your back. When it comes to what to plant, we don't pretend to be experts, but if, like us, you are a fair-weather gardener, we recommend plants that require minimum work yet offer maximum yield. In our top 10 list of easy-to-grow vegetables and flowers are cucumbers, cut-and-come-again lettuces, courgettes/zucchini, green beans, sugar snap peas, artichokes, dahlias, cosmos, sweet peas and the caviar of all home-grown veg, asparagus.

Opposite, clockwise from top left: artichokes growing rampantly in our vegetable plot; sugar snap peas growing in a scaffolding board bed with the builders' merchants name still visible on the side; there is nothing like fresh eggs laid by your own chickens; cut-and-come-again lettuces grown in an old enamel tub; beetroots plucked straight from the ground; in an old galvanized metal tub, large pebbles protect young cosmos seedlings from the predatory claws of our cats.

ALFRESCO LIVING

Outdoor living should be easy and fun. The wide wrap-around deck at our beach house has plenty of space for garden furniture, meaning that an impromptu meal in the garden is always an effortless affair (left). An old galvanized metal bathtub sits in a secluded corner of the garden surrounded by lush ferns for a luxurious, alfresco bathe. A vintage shower head is used to fill the bath up (below). Cooking outside is always an enjoyable way of getting back to nature. A huge paella sizzles away on the barbecue, and as night falls guests can perch on the log stools around it to keep warm (opposite).

Whether it's fish and chips wrapped in newspaper or a relaxed family barbecue, cooking and eating alfresco brings a deep sense of wellbeing.

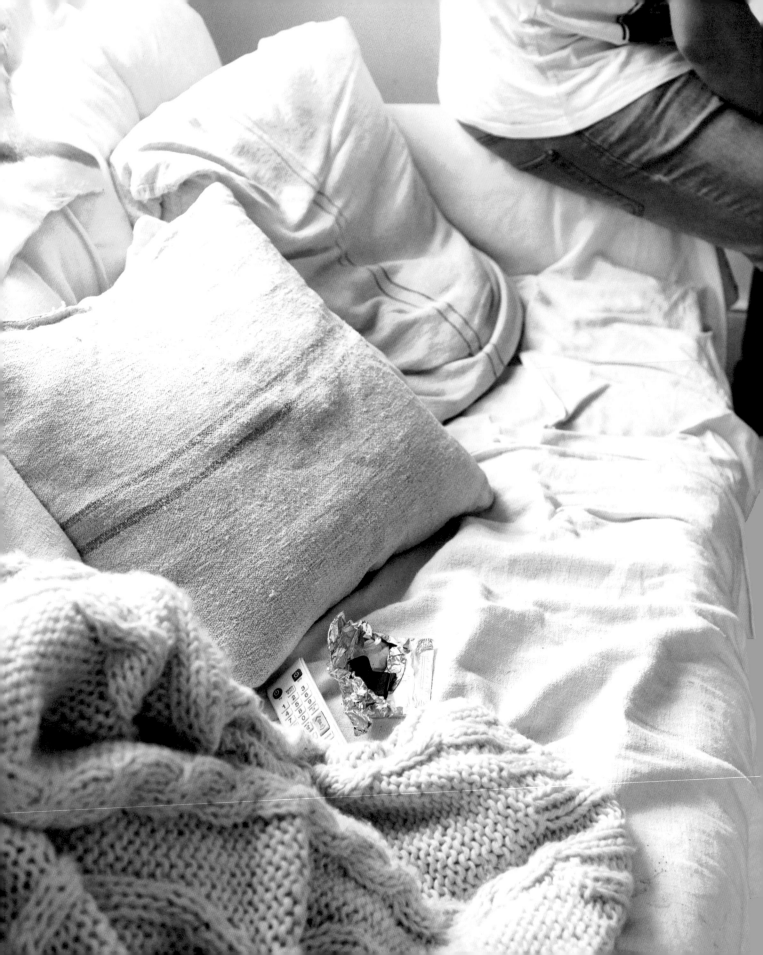

RELAX & ENJOY YOURSELF

Your home is your haven, a place to relax, unwind, play with the kids, enjoy the company of friends and be inspired. We think that no house is a design success if it does not meet the above criteria. Forget matching fabrics and untouchable antiques, and learn to enjoy imperfection. This is a laid-back approach to decorating that embraces family life and ensures that your house works for you, not the other way around.

Think carefully about the realities of your lifestyle and decorate your house accordingly. If you have young kids, then rather than stressing out every time they go near the sofa, make sure your loose covers are made from the kind of fabric that can be thrown in the washing machine on a regular basis. Similarly, floors should be hardwearing and easy to clean – no fluffy white carpets here! The idea is that if you make practical choices right from the start, you will be able to enjoy your home rather than being a slave to it. Of course, that doesn't mean that we are suggesting you compromise on style – far from it. Rather, we advocate that you embrace a style of decorating that can weather the bumps and scuffs of daily life while improving with age and growing in character.

DOWNTIME

There are certain areas of your home where it is essential that you allow yourself a little luxury. We're talking squashy sofas, comfy armchairs and cloud-like pillows. While metal tables and bare boards are hardworking on both a visual and practical level, when it comes to your downtime what you want is comfort.

A sofa will probably be your biggest financial outlay, so it is the one item in your house where a more conservative eye is needed: classic lines that won't date are the way to go, as you want it to last a long time. Antique leather armchairs look the business, but make sure the springs are sound and the leather is in good condition before you hand over your cash. Consider creating a snug corner by a window or near the fire where you can take a break and read a book in peace or, better still, fit out the shed at the bottom of the garden as your own private retreat.

A cosy library corner with a huge picture window is the ideal place to unwind (above). This living room is the perfect example of laid-back chic, with blowzy vintage florals offset by pastel-coloured industrial-style lighting, weathered floorboards and painted furniture (opposite). An old Victorian Chesterfield sofa has been given a relaxed makeover with loose covers made from antique linen sheets. Just the spot for a slice of lemon meringue pie.

A simple workbench has been created to look like an old potting table in this painter's retreat. Works in progress are pinned casually to the wall, while linen curtains at the window help to control the light on sunny days.

GET CREATIVE

Scientists have proved that having a creative interest outside your everyday life relieves stress, prevents depression, improves your memory and forces you to take a break, so strangely it can be more beneficial to those who are too busy as opposed to those who are twiddling their thumbs.

Whatever your interests – sewing, painting or playing a musical instrument – you will need somewhere to do it. Of course, there's nothing wrong with the kitchen table, but if you have the space, a designated room where you can lock yourself away and really lose yourself in a project is a great idea. The first things to consider when planning a work space are a table, chair and daylight. Old-fashioned trestle tables are perfect, as they are large and sturdy enough to spread out on, but if space is at a premium don't let that put you off – squeeze a little fold-down desk onto the landing or under the stairs.

Vintage blanket cushion covers

Transforming old woollen blankets into cushion covers is a great way to give them a new lease of life. Vintage Welsh blankets come in a variety of appealing colours and patterns. Classic designs have simple stripes in blue or pink at one end, while traditional pointing blankets often have broad, brightly coloured stripes at each end, which means that you may be able to make a selection of plain and striped cushion covers out of one blanket. Some have an attractive blanket stitch or satin edge, so try incorporating these into the design of your cover to create a decorative envelope opening at the back. Simple ties or a couple of chunky mother-of-pearl buttons will add a nice touch. Pretty one-colour dyed blankets are also available, or you could consider dyeing one of the plain cream or off-white varieties yourself, remembering to use cold water dyes to avoid felting the wool.

RUBBING ALONG TOGETHER

Family homes are hardworking – they have to be all things to all people. Kids need somewhere to play, teenagers need a place to do homework and grown-ups need a spot to relax and unwind in, not to mention somewhere you can all gather in the evening. If you have young kids, an open-plan arrangement is best to allow you to keep an eye on them at all times. Make sure there is plenty of toy storage so that tidying up before bedtime is quick and easy and you can enjoy a glass of wine once the children are asleep. Old metal trunks and baskets (the type with lids and leather buckles) make roomy toy boxes that are attractive enough to have in a main living space. And don't think that your little darlings' works of art must be hidden away – prop them up alongside your favourite ornaments and they will complement each other perfectly! Life with teenagers is a different matter and you will all benefit from a second living area where they (or you) can retreat to for some privacy. Ultimately, though, the secret to a happy and relaxed family home is a laid-back attitude and a good sense of humour – you will need it!

Children's paintings jostle with a bunch of antique keys (above left). Paper flowers made as a Mother's Day gift take pride of place alongside a galvanized pot of 'Mind your own Business' (above centre). Tea and toast – the stuff that childhood memories are made of (above right). Rubbing along together is all about acceptance. Rather than being hidden away, children's toys are an integral part of this décor, with a floral wigwam taking centre stage (opposite).

ENTERTAINING

Entertaining friends is all too often seen as a stressful chore requiring a complicated menu, formal table settings and polished silver. Well, not the Keep it Simple way! The important thing to remember is that your friends have come to see you, not eat a gourmet meal (we go to restaurants for that), so keep the fare simple and easy to prepare. Instead, concentrate on a few finishing touches that you will enjoy doing and that will make the event memorable. We gave this relaxed candlelit party at the bottom of our garden a hunting lodge feel and had a great time playing with the theme. Rustic benches were strewn with cosy, wool cushions and fur throws, walnuts were left on the table for guests to crack with small hammers and a 'trash can' fire outside allowed pre-dinner drinks to be enjoyed on the lawn, even though the evening was chilly (this page and opposite).

For a stress-free evening, keep the food simple and the atmosphere relaxed, allowing yourself the time to add a few finishing touches that will make it a memorable event.

MAKING IT
HAPPEN

Designing your perfect home.

THE BONES

Good 'bones' are essential if you want your house to be practical, functional and, of course, a thing of beauty, so getting the structural elements right will ensure that all the rest falls into place relatively easily. For us, reclamation yards are a great source of inspiration. Often a random find, such as a beautiful old door or salvaged wood panelling, can be the starting point for the design of an entire room, while something as tiny as the detail on a piece of moulding could become a theme that runs throughout an entire interior.

If you're renovating a period property, a converted barn or an ex-industrial space, you may be lucky enough to be working with great bones already. If so, you could consider the idea of 'undecorating' the space by stripping back partitions or walls to reveal the building's original structure, such as joists, beams or rafters. You will be amazed at what you can find beneath the plasterboard, and any elements that tell the story of the building's history can then be incorporated into your scheme.

However, if your house is lacking in character because it is a new build or a previous owner stripped out all its history, don't be afraid to put some personality back in by changing the doors, windows and architectural mouldings. Remember the space above your head too. You might think that cladding a low ceiling in faux beams and wooden planking might make it seem lower, but in fact the opposite is true.

WINDOWS & DOORS

If you are embarking on any structural work, spare some time and thought for windows and doors. Often taken for granted, they play a vital role in the look and mood of an interior and offer an opportunity to play with proportion, light and style. Salvage yards are a great place to source doors if you are working on a restoration project. Industrial styles can also work to great effect, sometimes adding a softer 'modern' feel where contemporary designs, such as wall-to-wall sliding glass doors, might seem too harsh. Sash windows always look elegant, but casements are more affordable and can work in a variety of situations. Ultimately, your aim is to flood the interior with as much daylight as possible.

Huge, salvaged antique glass doors, a round window in the eaves and large skylights all maximize the daylight in this spacious, double-height living room (above). Frosted engraved glass panels, rescued from an old pub, have been used to make a pair of elegant doors for a pretty en-suite bathroom, providing privacy while allowing light to flow from room to room (above right). Playing with styles and proportion can set the look of your home. Here, a single garage door has been used to lend a hint of industrial chic to our wooden beach house (opposite).

WALLS & PANELLING

Texture is an indispensable tool in the decorating of your home. It brings interest, contrast and depth in a way that no other element can. When it comes to adding texture to an interior, walls offer endless possibilities. Smooth plastered walls provide the perfect base for favourite paint colours, but don't rule out leaving the plaster bare (you can get plaster in pink or white), as it has a wonderful soft texture and hue all of its own, and sometimes an amazing crumbling plaster wall can be revealed behind old wallpaper that is too good to cover up.

Panelling and wood cladding are also hugely versatile, offering a wide range of surface finishes and styles. Rough sawn timber, elegant French-style panelling, understated tongue and groove or rustic planking fixed horizontally or vertically will all lend a different look and feel to a room.

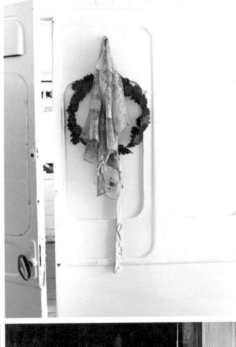

This crumbling plaster wall in a 17th-century French farmhouse hasn't been touched in decades out of choice rather than neglect (opposite). Half-cut logs have a simplicity that feels warm and rustic yet surprisingly modern (above left). The windows of the railway carriage/railroad car this home has been built around have been boarded up and painted to create a quirky style of panelling (above right). This hallway has been stripped back to reveal the structure of the boxed-in staircase behind (below right). Simple planking, used both vertically and horizontally, creates enough interest so that no beadhead is needed (below left).

FLOORS

A relaxed home demands that whatever you lay under your feet is not too precious. What's called for here is tough, workaday flooring that will stand the test of time and age well. Delicate, high-gloss finishes, pale carpets and anything high maintenance is vetoed.

Floors are the hardest-working element of any interior in more ways than one. Not only do they have to withstand a constant stream of traffic but they can also be used as a way to visually divide areas or provide continuity from one room to the next. On top of all that, the floor is also one of the most important components stylistically, as the sheer size of its surface area will dominate any space. Simple, honest materials are the way forward, with scrubbed or painted wooden floorboards, concrete or stone at the top of the list.

Light wooden flooring

Wooden boards treated with lye and white soap are our 'go-to' choice when it comes to flooring. A traditional treatment in Scandinavia, the finish is extremely durable yet has a soft, chalky texture and wears in a gentle, even way. Best of all, perhaps, the only maintenance needed is a mop with white soap once a week. Our floors have suffered plenty of red wine spillages, dropped food and dancing, yet after a couple of moppings any marks will disappear. Apply the lye (always wear protective gloves and goggles) to freshly sanded pine boards, brushing in the direction of the grain. Two coats can be applied if a lighter finish is required. Lye bleaches the wood and prevents yellowing. It also opens the grain, so at this stage the floor is susceptible to staining. Once it is dry, apply three coats of high-resolution white soap to seal. Always double check the manufacturer's instructions, as they can vary.

Old scaffolding boards, complete with scuffs, scrapes and old paint, make a hardwearing floor that will suit modern and period interiors alike (opposite). This polished concrete floor is both beautiful and robust (this page). The sheen of the surface helps to maximize the Italian sunshine that streams through the glass doors.

LIGHTING

Don't make the mistake of leaving lighting decisions to the end of your project. The way you plan to light your interior will need proper consideration so that you can instruct the electrician on the positioning of light fixtures and power sockets at an early stage. If you haven't decided on the style of the lights, just make sure you know where you want them, and if you're unsure, throw in a few extra sockets for table lamps.

You can change the feel of a room, adding a little glamour or industrial chic with the addition of a statement light. Clockwise from top left: an antique rise and fall has been given a modern edge with bright pink cord; add a touch of opulence with mercury glass shades; a factory table light has been reinvented as a wall light; a pretty mirror and crystal wall sconce brings sparkle; different-coloured cords can alter the look of any light; a 1950s glass lamp base lends a feminine touch; old Anglepoise lights are eternally stylish; chandeliers hint at decadence.

LAYOUT

Creating an accurate plan of your room is vital – it will give you a clear understanding of the space. In the early stages of your decorating project, think about how you want to use a space, especially if it has to be multitasking, such as a dining room-cum-study or a sitting room that's a through-route to the kitchen. Different-sized rooms throw up different challenges. In a small room, for instance, you will be trying to work out how to fit in the necessary furniture without the space feeling crowded, while a large room needs careful planning when it comes to furniture placement to avoid an unwelcoming 'warehouse' feel. The brilliant thing about drawing up a plan on paper is that you can disassociate yourself from how the room is currently laid out and let your imagination run free.

Planning your layout

There are many apps and websites that will enable you to create a layout of your home, but we still like to do it the old-fashioned way — on paper! Start by taking accurate measurements and creating a drawing of the basic outline of the space. A scale rule is a must (unless you happen to be a good mathematician), as it allows you to scale down your measurements to fit the piece of paper you are working on. Make sure that you mark down the correct positions and sizes of all the existing windows, doors, radiators and power sockets in the space and add any sweeps (the space needed to open doors). Create cut-out shapes to represent the furniture that you plan to put in the room (obviously these will need to scaled down by the same amount as the plan you have created) and you can then play around and try out varying furniture arrangements, lighting positions and possible structural changes on paper.

Zoning is very important when arranging the layout of one large open-plan space. One trick is to use furniture as room dividers to clearly delineate the different areas.

ARCHITECTURAL DETAILS

All too often, details such as architectural mouldings, skirting/baseboards, cornices and ceiling treatments are not thought through or are simply left for builders/contractors to sort out. If Charles Eames is to be believed, then 'Details are not details. They make the design', so architectural features such as these are an important and integral part of any successfully designed home and need attention at the early stages of a project.

Architraves and skirting/baseboards can help to alter the proportions and style of an interior. For instance, ornate, tall or deep versions of these will lend an air of grandeur and can even make a room seem taller or larger, while plainer designs (or even none at all) might feel more modern or rustic. Salvage yards are useful, as you can often find gems such as over-sized corbels, old shutters and antique hardware that you can incorporate into the fabric of your home.

Antique French shutters have been used to create a built-in cupboard, while beams have been exposed and painted white to bring interest to a low ceiling (above). Opposite, clockwise from top left: It's all in the detail. Salvaged from an old shop door, this brass handle has been turned on its side and fitted to the door of an integrated dishwasher; antique locks are so beautifully made that they are a feature in themselves; vintage-style light switches complete the look; antique plaster mouldings; huge wooden corbels support a shelf laden with heavy fossils and plaster casts; an old train door has been recommissioned for domestic use.

COLOUR

Without a doubt the most emotive element of any interior, colour plays an important role in the décor of your home. It is often considered the most daunting aspect of decorating (it's the thing we get asked about the most), which is odd when you consider that when it comes to colour there are no rights or wrongs, just personal taste. However, there are a few facts that could be useful when embarking on a decorating scheme and might help you navigate your way around paint charts and fabric swatches.

Firstly, colour is a brilliant device for altering the proportions of a space. Light, cool colours will visually push walls away, making a room seem bigger, for example, while warmer, darker colours will bring them in and prevent a large room from feeling empty and unfriendly.

There are three options when choosing a colour scheme. A tonal scheme uses colours that are from the same main group but in varying shades. A harmonious scheme pairs up colours that sit next to each other on the colour wheel, such as green and blue. And a contrasting scheme combines colours that sit opposite each other on the colour wheel and offset each other in a complementary way. Once you get to grips with these concepts, you can start to experiment and have fun with colour.

Lastly, colour is a brilliant device for pulling together apparently disparate components in an interior. For instance, a set of mismatched dining chairs could all be painted in either tonal, harmonious or contrasting shades for very different effects, while a house can be lent a balanced rhythm if every room is decorated in similar shades throughout.

NEUTRALS

Never bland, never boring, neutrals have a soft, soothing quality that will give any room a calming energy.

The best neutrals are natural materials: wood, linen, clay and stone. Texture is key when it comes to this gentle palette, so think of these materials as your best friends – their surface qualities will add depth and definition to any scheme.

Dark or light accents such as charcoal or white are also indispensable in a neutral scheme, as they prevent the shades blending into each other and

provide valuable contrast. If you have chosen taupe walls, then make sure you offset them with some touches of light and dark shades in the form of soft furnishings or flooring.

Paint isn't the only way to add colour to your walls. Old scaffolding boards make great wall cladding, as their uneven texture and weathered tones offer just the right neutral background. Natural fabrics have much to offer the neutral palette. Leather, hemp and hessian are all perfect choices, while driftwood, antlers and shells make great accessories. To finish off, include a little sparkle with some twinkly glass and add touches of just one strong colour like chartreuse, teal or fuschia – just as Mother Nature would do in the natural world.

In a neutral scheme, texture is needed to bring warmth and character. Decorative plaster walls and old stone give stark white walls interest (opposite above left). Natural finds make the perfect accessories (opposite right and below left). Subtle splashes of colour will lift a neutral palette (this page).

WHITES AND GREYS

Elegant, sophisticated and easy to live with, whites and greys are the perfect match. Whether you are decorating a modern masterpiece, a country cottage or a city apartment, these two unassuming hues can come together to create a sublime combination that is quiet yet uplifting. Stick to a simple two-shade palette for a monochrome look that is much easier to live with than classic black and white, or mix and blend a whole array of varying shades from charcoal and slate through to alabaster and pebble for a more subtle effect.

French antique linen sheets that have been dyed using Dylon's Antique Grey are used here to cover the sofa and cushions and lend our cosy snug an elegant feel. White tongue-and-groove panelling on the walls freshens the look, while lime green hydrangeas and shocking pink cord on the rise and fall light add just the right hint of colour (previous pages). A charcoal padded headboard and a slate grey linen throw look clean and modern against whitewashed walls (this page). In this bathroom, dark grey walls are lifted with accents of white (opposite above left). The Little Greene Paint Company's French Grey has been used on the floors, walls and kitchen cabinets in this pretty kitchen by the sea (opposite above right). An old factory workbench makes an unusual kitchen island.

Neither black nor white, grey draws little attention to itself yet complements everything around it. It has an appealing dual personality, as it evokes images of beautiful, winter beach scenes as much as it does gritty, industrial environments.

What's amazing about these two magic colours is that they can evoke such a vast array of moods and styles. Warm tones such as mink, mouse and lime white create a luxurious and cosy feel. Stark white and steel grey will conjure a much cleaner modern vibe; French or Swedish greys, on the other hand, will instantly lend a room some chic finesse.

For a contemporary interior, grey walls are the perfect backdrop for bolder accents of colour. Yellow, acid greens, turquoise and pinks all work particularly well. Grey can be also introduced in other ways by choosing furniture and accessories in soft shades of granite or stone and offsetting them against off-white walls.

VINTAGE PASTELS

Gone are the days when pastels were confined to the baby's nursery. They have a soothing, hazy quality that is soft and welcoming but will lend an elegant twist to any interior. Their desaturated character means that they can be treated almost as neutrals, blended and layered without them jarring. The danger, however, is that too much of them and a room becomes sweet and saccharine. To avoid this, include lots of pure white and plenty of negative (empty) space. Introducing harder elements, such as wood and metal, will also ensure that you get the balance just right.

A stark white sofa creates a blank canvas for showing off vintage floral cushion covers, while the rough-planked walls act as a foil to the pretty decorative elements, giving the room a simple rustic charm (previous pages). Pastel colours work particularly well on metal, as this powder blue enamel stove demonstrates (opposite). A selection of mismatched vintage dinner plates (right). Plenty of white space surrounds an odd assortment of painted garden chairs and shows that pastels can be pretty but not sickly (far right).

Dyeing antique linen sheets

We love antique linen sheets. Not only do they make instant curtains, sofa covers and bedspreads but they also dye wonderfully well. This is a useful attribute if you have any antique sheets with stubborn old stains that you can't shift. Pure white linen will take your chosen shade in a true way to give clean, fresh colour, but slubby hemp sheets will emerge from the dye vat with a softer, more mottled hue that is just as pleasing. Unbleached Metis sheets, on the other hand, already have a creamy colour to them that will serve to knock back any chosen dye colour to a more earthy hue. One thing is for sure, though: no two sheets will ever come out identical, which we think is all part of the charm.

Making your own natural dyes is great fun (there are plenty of websites that will show you how) and it is amazing what vibrant colours can be achieved from humble plants such as nettles, beetroot or berries, but if that seems too much of a faff, then shop-bought dyes come in a good range of colours and are extremely simple and easy to use.

BOLD ACCENTS

We all have colours that
make our heart sing – shades
that make us smile and lift our
spirits. However, none of us
wants to be saturated in that
colour – too much of any one
thing can be overwhelming.
The idea is to inject small
pops of just one or two bright
colours against a neutral or
white backdrop. Not only will
this punctuate the room and
provide something to rest your
eye on, it will also give you
a chance to express your
personality and create your
own individual look.

If working with strong
colour is something that
frightens you, then start with
small doses: cushions, vases,

Clothes are a brilliant way of introducing colour into a bedroom. Fashion is faster-paced and more transient than interior design, meaning you can ring the changes frequently and be more frivolous with your injections of colour. A row of hooks provides a perfect backdrop against which to display favourite items (previous page). A turquoise door gives just the right pop of colour to lift the spirits (this page).

Think carefully about what colours make you happy. Take inspiration from your wardrobe or garden, as they will undoubtedly tell a story of the colours you are naturally drawn to.

pictures, lighting or a painted chair are all great ways to add a shot of your favourite shade. Perhaps you already possess some treasured objects that you would like to use as the basis for your accent palette, such as a vintage dress or a lamp you inherited from your grandmother.

If you are feeling brave, try creating an accent wall or perhaps upholstering a sofa or armchair for a bolder statement. The trick is to keep things balanced: every bold piece should be countered with something neutral or white. And remember to keep to a restricted palette of just one or two accent colours.

Saris are wonderfully vibrant. Throw them over a sofa or bed, or hang them as floaty curtains. Keep everything else plain and white for a contemporary look (above left). Vintage 1950s and '60's glass in delicious jewel-like tones stands out against a white backdrop (above).

FURNITURE

There is more to choosing a piece of furniture than just falling in love with an item at first sight; it has to be practical too. Luckily, in the Keep it Simple home this isn't a problem, as in our eyes the most beautiful examples are the ones in which form follows function.

Very few of us start out designing a room that's a completely blank canvas. Usually, we will be working with items that we already own – previous purchases that have to be incorporated due to financial restraints, or much-loved family heirlooms that it would be unthinkable to live without. Don't worry, though; matching three-piece suites are not the way to a relaxed and happy home. Practicality, individuality and comfort are what we are striving for. However, to make your quest a little easier, here are some guidelines to ensure your furniture choices are good ones.

Firstly, construction should be solid. Sadly, this is not the case with many cheaper, mass-produced designs, and good-quality pieces tend to be expensive. Scour junk shops and auctions for vintage pieces made using old techniques and built to last. Secondly, when it comes to looks, clean lines and classic styles are a good way to go. A piece of furniture is a big investment, and you need it to stand the test of time.

Finish is the one element that you can really play around with. Whether it's those dining chairs you are sick of the sight of or an armchair your great-aunt left you, sometimes a lick of paint or some new seat cushions and upholstery might be all they need to bring them back into favour.

SEATING

It should go without saying that seating must be comfortable, but there are some other considerations to bear in mind. Sofas and armchairs can look bulky, so opt for leggy models, which look more elegant. Dining chairs should be easy to clean: food and upholstery are not good partners, so wipeable materials such as wood and metal are preferable. If you like seat pads, make sure the covers are washable. And don't believe that dining chairs all have to match; an eclectic mix will add to the relaxed vibe.

Stools are useful in the kitchen. If you have a central island, guests will love perching there while you get on with the cooking, and a mismatched selection of different heights will cater for everyone.

Don't be too precious. Sofas and armchairs should invite guests and family members to sit down and relax, so overstuffed cushions that they are too scared to make a dent in or upholstery that shouts 'keep off' are definitely out. Instead, opt for relaxed lines, loose covers that can be thrown in the washing machine and cushions that positively beg to be sunk into (above and opposite). Footstools make useful occasional seating when bodies outnumber seats, and they will also do double duty as somewhere comfy to put your feet up (above right). Make sure you cover them in a hardwearing fabric that won't show the dirt easily.

'Don't make something unless it is both necessary and useful; but if it is both necessary and useful, don't hesitate to make it beautiful.' So said the Shakers, and we couldn't agree more, as our favourite pieces usually have utilitarian origins. This page, clockwise from top left: this Gaston Viort aluminium café chair was designed as part of a post-war movement by aircraft manufacturers to find other uses for their factories; a vintage railway/railroad station bench has a simplicity that still feels fresh today; these early 1950s canvas and steel stacking chairs were originally designed for municipal use; an elegant vintage French park chair; this wooden milking stool is simple and handy; a gorgeous mid-20th-century metal stool. An antique Swedish bench is both beautiful and useful and complements the French country table perfectly (opposite). Communal seating around a long dining table is a great way to create a relaxed, laid-back vibe.

THE KITCHEN TABLE

In most modern houses it's the hub of the home; the centre of gravity around which everything happens, from homework and haircuts to breakfast and dinner parties. Go for something sturdy, scrubbable and as big as your space will allow. Old rectory or farmhouse tables should be tough enough to take all the knocks, scuffs and spillages that your family can throw at them while also being aesthetically pleasing. Or you could create your own with a couple of trestles and some chunky scaffolding planks on top. Paint them white or charcoal grey, or bleach them for a natural, beachy look.

OCCASIONAL TABLES

Often overlooked, occasional tables are one of the most hardworking pieces of furniture in the home. Although not designed with any particular use in mind, the demands on them are multiple – we use them to display flowers, lamps, books and just to put a cup of coffee down on. It's no wonder then that they are actually quite pivotal in pulling a room scheme together.

Console tables are particularly valuable for providing a surface on which to create a focal point or vignette in a room. A slimmed-down trestle table will do the trick, or hunt down antique wrought-iron garden table bases and top them with marble or planks of wood. Side tables give you a chance to get creative; try old cases stacked on top of each other, wooden crates turned on their sides or even a chunky log might just fit the bill.

Making a table from a vintage mirror

Adding sparkle and glamour to any interior, antique Venetian mirrored furniture is a collectible commodity that commands high prices. Modern versions are available, but they don't have the patina and elegance of the originals. Instead, why not try creating a small side table using a vintage 20th-century mirror, which are more readily available. They come in a variety of shapes and sizes and often have pretty bevelled edges or engravings. Simply remove the metal clasps that hold the mirror to the ply backing and set them to one side. Next, fix some legs to the back of the ply with wood glue and screws. If you are keen on woodwork, you could fashion these yourself. If not, upholstery suppliers tend to stock a varied selection of chair legs, or perhaps you might want to mount the backing plate onto a rustic log stump for an eclectic look. Once you have the base fixed to your backing plate, you can then re-fix your mirror to the ply with the clips you saved earlier.

Old munitions boxes have been stacked to create an attractive side table that doubles up as storage (opposite). A wrought-iron and marble console table creates a focal point and offers a chance to add some decorative elements to this simple scheme (this page). An old French mirror contrasts with a galvanized bucket that holds a vibrant blue hydrangea. Quails' eggs in glass vases contribute texture and a natural element to the theme.

CUPBOARDS & DRESSERS

There is no such thing as too much storage, and if you have done your homework right, you will have installed plenty of built-in storage at the early stages of your home renovation. However, there is always a place for freestanding pieces.

Dressers/hutches have a wonderful cottagey feel and present the opportunity to simultaneously display and store a prized china and glass collection, as do glazed book cabinets, which needn't be confined to the library. If you like the idea of mixing it up, an elegant armoire would look fabulous in a sleek, modern kitchen to house food or cooking equipment. In the living room, low-level cupboards also provide a surface on which to place decorative objects or a

lamp, and an old metal and glass medicine cabinet could add some industrial chic while also showing off your favourite treasures. Salvaged haberdashery shop and museum fittings can look stylish, and reclamation yards are the place to hunt them down. Old metal school lockers are perfect in the hallway to hold coats, hats and shoes and other assorted bits and pieces, while an antique linen press would work in just about any room in the house. Finally, mirrored-door armoires make stunning centrepieces in any room – they bounce lots of light around, which helps to make a small space feel bigger.

When we found this dresser in a junk shop in South London it was bright orange and had a horrible Formica top. Now painted white and situated in one of our lovely cabins, it looks as if it has always been there (opposite). The pale Swedish blue colour of this huge cupboard belies its bulk and boxiness and tranforms it into something light and pretty (left). A matching pair of antique linen presses provides ample storage space and their positioning creates a cosy nook that is home to a pretty vignette of vintage pictures and a rustic bowl on a French antique garden table (above).

BEDS & DAY BEDS

Whether you want your bedroom to be a calming, tranquil space or you prefer to be surrounded by decorative accessories, your bed should reflect your chosen style.

Cast-iron bedsteads have a romantic feel that suit both simple country interiors and feminine boudoirs, while French carved wooden bedsteads exude elegance. If you want to make a more personal statement, mix it up a little. An ornate upholstered antique bed would look contemporary in a bare, monastic room, whereas a cast-iron bedstead could be given a modern twist with a coat of charcoal paint.

Day beds might seem like a luxury that nobody has space for, but why not replace your sofa with one, piled with cushions, for the ultimate in decadent TV viewing.

An antique Indian bed makes an elegant focal point in a living room. Vintage linens and mattress ticking have been used to create a luxurious spot for lounging (above). Cast-iron beds work in both traditional and contemporary interiors (above right). Reeded wood panelling painted in a pretty vintage shade (Cupboard Green by The Little Greene Paint Company) boxes in a fitted day bed in an Airstream trailer that serves as a guest bedroom. Bedding can be stowed away under the mattress when the bed is not in use, and scatter cushions transform it into an inviting sofa by day (opposite).

FABRICS

Fabrics are your chance to make a mark in terms of personal style, but it can be an intimidating task wading through fabric swatches – the wide variety of textures, weights, compositions and patterns available can be a little overwhelming.

The best place to start, then, is by thinking about the kind of mood you are trying to evoke, as different fabrics will produce different effects. For instance, linen slipcovers with a slightly crumpled, relaxed feel create a light, airy look that is reminiscent of a Long Island beach house, while generous floor-length curtains printed with full-blown roses conjure up images of an English country house. Having said that, the way in which you put your chosen fabrics to use will also have an impact on their final effect. That same linen used on a more formal, upholstered chair might give the feel of an elegant Parisian apartment, while the traditional English chintz could be used to provide a contemporary pop of colour on a modern sofa in an all-white room. The point is to have some fun with it. So-called experts might spout gobbledygook about the rules of drapery vs upholstery fabrics, but as we all know rules were made to be broken (with the possible exception of seating fabrics in high-traffic areas), so feel free to use that thick blanketing at the windows or that pretty linen sprig on your favourite armchair.

ANTIQUE LINENS

We can't get enough of antique linens. They have a texture, drape and durability rarely found in their modern counterparts. We use them to make tablecloths, curtains, sofa and cushion covers and bed linen, and have been known to piece together badly torn sheets to make loose covers. Antique sheets made of plain hemp drape the most beautifully, as they are heavy and loosely woven. Sheets made from flax linen often have meticulously hand-stitched monograms and feature decorative threadwork. Their thread count is usually higher than hemp sheets, giving them a more refined feel. Metis sheets, made from a mixture of cotton and linen, tend not to be as old, and although hardwearing, they don't drape quite as well.

Grain sacks make great no-sew cushion covers (opposite). Ever versatile, antique linen has been used to cover the chair and cushion, as well as to make simple roll-up blinds at our beach house (right).

Grain sacks

It's not just their good looks and strength that make grain sacks so desirable. For us, it's also the combination of personal history and utilitarian heritage. Usually dating from around the 1850s to the early 1900s, their manufacture was a homespun affair, from growing the flax or hemp to the spinning of the yarn, the weaving of the fabric and the sewing of the final sack. Every stage took place on the family farm , and each farmer added a unique coloured stripe to his sacks for identification. As we prefer not to cut the sacks in order to keep the original, tiny hand stitches, we use them to make table runners, bathmats, cushions covers, laundry bags and pillowcases, but the thickness of their fabric does make them ideal for upholstery. Luckily, it is possible to source grain-sack material by the metre/yard, which saves us the sad task of ever cutting into these beautiful pieces of history.

VINTAGE PATTERNS

From the pretty French sprigs of the 1800s and voluptuous 1930s florals to more recent stylized 1950s prints and bold geometric designs of the 1970s, there is a vintage pattern to suit every home. Whether you use them in tiny touches or great swathes, they can bring an individuality and charm that the mass-produced fabrics of today can't quite provide. It's not always easy to find large quantities of the same design, but when it comes to vintage florals this shouldn't matter, as a little goes a long way. One single patterned cushion among four plain ones might be just enough to bring your sofa to life, and a single metre/yard of 1940s dress fabric would be perfect pinned up at a small window. But if you are lucky enough to come across a larger length of a gorgeous, linen union strewn with blowzy roses, then be bold and use it to cover a sofa or armchair.

Pale pink and powder-blue 19th-century French country cottons have been made into pretty pillowcases (this page). Opposite, clockwise from top left: don't be afraid to mix up patterns from different eras. Here, an American 1920s cotton floral sits happily with a bolder 1940s dress fabric; sometimes a tiny scrap of fabric is enough to cover a small window; 1950s barkcloth has a wonderful texture that is very distinctive; mixing a few different designs together creates an eclectic look, but tempering various patterns with lots of white calms everything down.

Mixing fabrics that seem as if they would be at odds with one another not only helps you to develop your own signature look but also creates a relaxed feel that is stylish without looking as if you have tried too hard. It's the sense of contrast that holds the allure, as luxurious fabrics dress up more practical textiles, while the rougher, more durable ones will, in turn, bring their glamorous sisters down to earth. This page, clockwise from top left: layers of wool and linen make for a cosy sofa; hessian and calico tame the luxury of silk damask and sheepskin; a laid-back knit is thrown across the arm of a gilt chair; an antique hand-embroidered silk sari lifts this tatty leather chair out of dereliction; antique linen is mixed with sumptuous sheepskin for a luxe effect; an 18th-century embroidered bedspread brings an aura of glamour to white linen sheets. Chunky knits and furs are the perfect foil for an antique Italian gilt sofa that might otherwise look a little 'bling' (opposite).

TEXTURE

Fabrics are the perfect way to introduce texture into your home. Chunky knits, tactile embroidery, soft furs and slippery satin will all bring textural variety into your scheme by adding definition and sensuality.

Luxurious fabrics like velvet, leather and fur would traditionally be associated with a more formal interior, while workaday textiles such as wool, denim and cotton have a more casual look. Layering fabrics that have a contrasting texture is a great way to get the most out of them, so combine fluffy with rough – angora and hessian, for example – or shiny with matt – like silk damask and suede – for maximum effect. Think leather sofas strewn with crushed velvet cushions, beds piled with vintage blankets, pillow-soft eiderdowns and crisp cotton sheets and armchairs covered in slubby linen and draped in fur throws. You get the idea.

DETAILS & ACCESSORIES

Once you have got the structure, paintwork and furnishings of your home in place, you can start to have fun with the finishing touches. Vases, pictures, small soft furnishings and objets d'art are perfect opportunities for you to express yourself and allow you to make your mark in a more frivolous, transient way that can vary depending on your mood, the current season or passing trends.

Cushions and throws are one of the easiest items to refresh and can change the whole look of a room. Don't be afraid to mix on-trend chain-store purchases with treasured family heirlooms and more expensive made-to-measure or hand-crafted items, as this will help your scheme stay up to the minute while also preserving a sense of individuality.

Changing things around according to the seasons is a great way to keep your home feeling fresh. Floor rugs, textured throws, vases in darker shades, candlesticks and winter flower displays can transform a light, summery room into a cosy den for the colder months. On the other hand, bowls of shells, pretty chintzy cushions, gossamer-light curtains and bare floors will make the same room feel ready for spring. The secret to success is to not have all your prized possessions out on show at any one time – after all, you would never wear all your jewellery at once. Instead, be selective and edit your items, only showing a few at a time.

THE DECORATIVE LANDSCAPE

How you group and arrange your decorative elements is every bit as important as the actual items you are displaying – careful curation will ensure that they all have maximum impact without being overbearing. Texture, form, colour and scale all need to be balanced, but you will also require a hook or concept for your collection so that your visual theme can tell a story. This theme could be anything that appeals to you – nature, for example, or a colour, a collection of teacups or even items dating from an era you particularly love. Once you have grouped together three or four objects that are related, you will be able to go off-piste by adding a few items that don't strictly adhere to the theme – this will ensure that your arrangement is a personal expression rather than a museum display. Composition and placement is also vital. Little clusters of objects will add weight and drama to a decorative landscape, but make sure that you vary the heights, with smaller pieces at the front. Finally, pay attention to the negative (empty) space, as this will allow your collection to breathe.

Shadow boxes are a great way to display 3-D objects on the wall. Here, some brightly coloured butterflies add a dash of colour to the natural and monochrome themes (above left). Varying colours, forms and textures pull together a collection of antique and contemporary glass (above).

This vignette tells a story of faded grandeur, while the gentle colour palette of gold and blue keeps the overall effect light and feminine.

Huge fossils, corals and antlers all adhere to a natural theme, while balls of string, plaster casts and a marble carving help to consolidate this idea without the effect becoming laboured. Twinkly glass mirrors and an antique French paste votive add a sub-plot of glamour. The items have been grouped into clusters and pairs for maximum impact, with a variety of heights mimicking an undulating landscape across this richly encrusted mantelpiece.

MIRRORS

We just can't do without mirrors. Not because we're vain, as someone once suggested, but because they offer such brilliant solutions to a wide range of interior design problems. They reflect light into dark corners, make small spaces seem bigger, create vistas and focal points, add sparkle to a dull room and help to shape the look of an interior, depending on the style you choose. In addition, it is very hard to put on make-up without one! Oversized floor-to-ceiling mirrors can make a huge statement and work surprisingly well in small rooms, as they will lend a sense of elegance and serve to open up the space, while a collection of mismatched decorative mirrors hung in a hallway or over a sofa can imbue some individual character. Antique mirrors with a mottled patina and early mercury-backed examples are highly sought after, as their reflections have a soft, evocative quality that is hard to replicate.

A 1920s grey painted wooden mirror rescued from a panelled room in Paris that was being ripped out works hard to make this small, snug room feel much bigger than it actually is by creating the illusion of a vista through to another room (opposite above left). A collection of vintage mirrors from the early part of the 20th century creates a quirky arrangement (opposite above right). An antique window salvaged from a house in France has been glazed with reflective glass to create this elegant arched mirror (right).

FOUND OBJECTS

A home should be thought of as a living organism that alters and evolves over time, reflecting the changing lives and whims of its occupants, telling their stories, meeting their needs and charting their histories. A great way to ensure that your home fulfils this promise is to embrace the idea of using found objects.

These could be something as simple as a bowl full of conkers collected on a crisp autumn walk or a bundle of twigs displayed in a glass vase rather than flowers. How about starting a family tradition by collecting a handful of beach on every seaside holiday you take (but please check local laws in case the area is a protected environment). When you get home, put the sand, shells, shingle or whatever you picked up into a glass Kilner/canning jar, label it with the place and date that you collected its contents and display them all together on a shelf or dresser. Over a period of years you will build up a collection of jars that will tell the story of your family vacations just as much as any photo album could do.

Pebbles, shells and pine cones collected all over the world are displayed together in this vintage wooden box, telling the tale of trips and visits over the years (opposite). A piece of fisherman's rope found washed up on the beach has been put to good use as a curtain tie-back on this four-poster bed (above left). Garden blooms sit on the table waiting to be painted in this artist's studio (above centre). On stony beaches we have a family game to see who can find the first pebble with a hole in it. When we get home, any that are found are strung onto rope and hung up for decoration (above right).

FLOWERS

No home is complete without flowers, so whether it's an elegant tall-stemmed vase billowing with sky blue hydrangeas or just a simple glass jar of humble daffodils, try to have some on display somewhere. There is no mystery to flower arranging, just a matter of finding the right vessel for the right flower. The trick is to think about what each flower's best attribute is and find a container that will show off that feature. For instance, huge blowzy blooms such as roses and peonies can look stunning cut short and packed together in low, wide vases to showcase the generosity of their abundant petals. Willowy flowers like anemones can be displayed to their best advantage a few at a time in elegant glass bottles that will highlight their twisted stems. Tall, spire-like structures such as foxgloves or delphiniums will create a regal and architectural statement in a tall, straight-sided cylindrical vase. Learn to appreciate flowers in all their phases, as most will be just as beautiful in their final faded stages as they are in the first bloom of youth. Tulips seem to get better and better as their stems continue to grow into extravagant shapes and the colour of their petals darkens with age until they finally drop, while guelder roses morph from bouncy lime green pompoms through to full-blown, creamy white blooms that hang with weighty extravagance after a couple of weeks.

Simplicity is the best policy when it comes to arranging flowers, but always be bold and generous while remembering to keep an open mind to all forms of beauty.

QUALITY
FEEDS

MANUFACTURED BY
CENTRAL CO-OPERATIVE WHOLESALE
SUPERIOR, WIS.

Living in the Countrys

RALPH LAU

With flowers, as with so many things, we think it's best to keep it simple. Clockwise from top left: anemones showing off their elegant stems in old apothecary bottles; lavish peonies looking fabulous in a vintage French glass jar; pale blue aquilegias plucked from the garden make a great spring-time show; apple blossom looks perfect in a simple jar; buddleia make a big statement in a bell jar; one perfect camellia stem is all that is needed; a bucket full of dahlias has a casual extravagance; cutting the stems short on roses really helps to draw your attention to the beauty of the blooms.

LIVING THE DREAM

Relaxed rooms that work
for all the family.

SITTING ROOMS & COSY NOOKS

We all need somewhere to flop, a place where we can relax and chill out, but as many of us now have multifunctional, open-plan living rooms with kitchen, dining, lounging and entertaining all taking place in one big space, it's not always easy. That's why it is so important that we all have a corner somewhere dedicated to downtime. And regardless of whether you have a small separate sitting room or a lounging zone that's part of one large space, concentrating on the right elements will ensure that your haven has a laid-back, calming atmosphere.

The key feature will undoubtedly be the sofa, as this is likely to be the most dominant element in the room, but equally important is a focal point around which the seating can be arranged. Fireplaces are the perfect way to create a centrepiece, while the mantelpiece will provide a place for you to display favourite accessories and personalize the space. Wood-burning stoves also work well, and have the advantage of not being confined to the chimney breast, as you can fit a flue almost anywhere. They look great freestanding, surrounded by baskets of logs and kindling, and with the vast array of designs available, they should fit into just about any decorating scheme.

These days, it is often the TV that takes pride of place. Rather than fight it, go with it, but sit yours on something beautiful. A cabriole-legged console table or a vintage metal cabinet will do, or you could mount it on the wall, surrounded by works of art and posters so that it blends in.

Family momentos keep a living space personal, like this photograph taken by our son Indigo and a once-loved toy Spitfire (above left). The 1950s moulded blossom branch was found in a junk shop (above right). In the summer months, we stack our fireplace with logs (left). Shots of pink, lime and turquoise add colour to the greys and browns in this elegant sitting room (opposite). It's the mix of textures – leather, wood, metal – that make this such a comforting space.

Glazed doors close off this cosy corner from the rest of the room when privacy is needed. An antique linen sheet has been thrown over the sofa and acts as an impromptu loose cover for a laid-back and casual feel, while an eclectic mix of accessories keeps it light and personal (left). At our seaside cabin, the huge vaulted ceiling has been exposed and painted white to maximize the sense of light and space (opposite). However, the wood-burning stove, darker accents and relaxed furniture ensure that the space never feels cold and gaping, despite its lofty proportions. A bowl full of small decorative plaster casts adds some textural detail to a simple scheme (below).

As well as being your personal retreat, the living room is the most sociable room in the house and one where family and friends will gather, so a relaxed, welcoming feel is essential.

A stack of cut logs creates a rich, textural wall that brings colour and depth to this snug (opposite). Antique leather armchairs lend some masculine gravitas, whereas the cherry blossom lights and floral cushions add a feminine touch. A lesson in greys and whites, the pale colour scheme gives this tiny library a fresh and airy feel, while an array of varying sensual textures keeps it inviting (this page).

Natural wood and chunky textures will always ensure that an interior feels warm and welcoming. Rough sawn logs and corrugated iron have been used to clad the walls of this charming cabin in the grounds of our home to create a romantic hideaway apart from the main house (left). Vintage floral cushions prevent it from becoming too sombre and dark, while the iconic 1960s print of 'Tina' by J.H. Lynch, salvaged from Dave's family attic, adds some light-hearted humour. A rare English leather armchair dating from around 1900 is paired with an elegantly dishevelled Victorian slipper chair, and an old fishing-tackle box is used as a coffee table (opposite).

COOKING & EATING

Probably the most important room in the house, the kitchen is so much more than just a place to cook and eat – it's a centre of creativity, activity, socializing and nourishment. Never sedate or formal, it should be full of noise, cooking smells and energy, and as such it needs a décor to suit. Forget sleek lines or easily scratched surfaces that you will fret over; what we're talking about here is a functional yet easy-going space filled with robust furniture that can take all the abuse a busy family will inflict on it and which makes guests feel instantly welcome and at home.

The idea of a separate dining room is mostly obsolete now, as most modern homes will have a combined kitchen and eating area, not to mention using the space as an office, living room and laundry room too. Storage is going to be your number-one problem, so make sure you have plenty of it. Some things will need to be hidden away, while others you might want to make a feature of by stacking them on open shelves or in glazed cabinets. A big range cooker makes a wonderful centrepiece and will be tough enough to cope with all the catering that goes on in most family homes. And if you have the space, a kitchen island is a must, as it allows for extra work and storage capacity at the same time as offering a nice central focal point around which your friends and family can gather while you cook.

Honest materials and sturdy furniture give this kitchen a practical yet homely feel (opposite). White Delft tiles bounce light into the room, while the mantel surround creates the feel of an old-fashioned hearth and puts the cooker at the heart of the room. Containers full of fresh basil, asparagus and fennel picked from the vegetable garden sit on the window sill (above left). A cutting board has been fashioned out of an old floorboard (above). Fresh eggs laid by our hens sit in a bowl showing off a beautiful array of colours (left).

Rough textures and practical surfaces give this tiny kitchen, made almost entirely out of recycled materials, a robust quality that makes it seem larger than it really is (above left and left). The splashback was fashioned from a sheet of salvaged zinc and the kitchen island was once a science laboratory table in a school. The unfitted nature of this country kitchen creates a relaxed, informal atmosphere, yet the huge, decorative painted armoire adds a hint of feminine glamour (above and opposite). The family that live here use the vintage electric cooker in the summer months when their AGA range cooker is switched off.

Along the coasts of England, there is a tradition for old, disused railway carriages/railroad cars to be turned into houses. The form of this bespoke kitchen dresser/hutch shows quite clearly how the train carriage/car has been cleverly incorporated into its design (left). Skylights in the high-pitched roof flood our family kitchen with natural daylight (opposite). Industrial castors have been added to a simple French table with a zinc top, while open shelves offer a practical and attractive way to store tableware. A butler's sink makes a focal point under the window, offering a beautiful view of open countryside – an incentive to do the dish washing.

Sometimes it's nice to make an effort and really go to town with the decorations when entertaining. Here, a random selection of chairs has been pulled around two trestle tables covered with white linen tablecloths (this page). A treasured collection of mismatched vintage dinner plates that has been accumulated over the years, twinkly chandeliers, piles of cloud-like meringues and blowzy pink peonies all lend an air of pretty opulence. Unfitted kitchens have an honest simplicity that is true to our ethos and are the perfect way to showcase original vintage pieces like the 1950s fridge and 1940s Rayburn stove in this elegant yet rustic cooking space (opposite above and below)

Rhubarb & vanilla pavlova

FOR THE MERINGUE

8 egg whites; 450 g/2¼ cups caster/superfine sugar; a splash of white wine vinegar; 1 teaspoon cornflour/cornstarch

FOR THE TOPPING

1 vanilla pod/bean; 900 g/2 lb. rhubarb, chopped into 2.5-cm/1-in. chunks; 110 g/½ cup caster/superfine sugar; 1 tablespoon sweet sherry or marsala wine; 600 ml/2½ cups double/heavy cream, whipped to stiff peaks.

Preheat the oven to 140°C (285°F) Gas 1. For the meringue, whisk the egg whites until stiff. While still whisking, add the sugar, a spoon at a time, then the vinegar and then the cornflour/cornstarch. Heap blobs of the meringue mixture on to a greased and lined baking sheet. Bake for 1 hour in the preheated oven. Turn the oven off but leave the meringue in the oven until completely cold. Remove and set aside. Preheat the oven to 180°C (350°F) Gas 4. To make the topping, split the vanilla pod/bean lengthways, scrape out the seeds and place them in an ovenproof dish along with the rhubarb, sugar and sherry. Mix well, then bake in the preheated oven for 20 minutes. Let cool. To assemble, spoon whipped cream into the meringue case and top it with the rhubarb and juices.

A little imagination, a bold eye and a pile of salvaged materials are the perfect ingredients for a simple, rustic kitchen that won't break the bank.

The casual, deconstructed elements of this French farmhouse prove that you don't need to spend a fortune on a kitchen (above left). Rustic doors have been constructed out of reclaimed wood and a plain ceramic sink sits on top of the marble work surface, while the taps/faucets have been plumbed into a piece of salvaged panelling. The original stone shelves have been carefully retained and are as just good today as they were 300 or so years ago, when the house was built (above). The family who live in this beautiful French farmhouse still use the fireplace to cook on even now (left). An old workbench rescued from a disused factory makes a solid and striking central island (opposite).

SLEEPING & WASHING

Bedrooms and bathrooms should make you feel serene and rested. They should be dreamy places of tranquillity, offering an escape from the outside world and allowing us to concentrate on the private sides of our lives. Gentle, soothing shades will work best on the walls, so go for soft greys, cool whites and faded pastels, and introduce stronger colours in small doses using accessories. In the bedroom you might want to use clothes and jewellery for this purpose, so strategically placed hooks for a vintage gown or an antique glass cake stand to hold your jewellery would be perfect.

Bedding is another great way to introduce colour and interest, but don't fall into the trap of thinking you have to buy matching sets. Instead, try a more individual approach and combine white sheets with vintage floral pillowcases, feather eiderdowns, soft mohair throws in calming tones and cotton waffle blankets in muted hues. This same approach can be applied to the bathroom, so if possible avoid off-the-peg bathroom suites and go for a more eclectic look. Source an antique rolltop tub from a salvage yard or specialist bathroom shop and combine it with mini his-and-her butler's sinks on simple cast-iron brackets. You could even try reinventing an old enamel washtub as a basin.

Bathroom lighting is always tricky, as there are a limited number of designs that are suitable. We often opt for garden lights for bathrooms, and old nautical designs are always worth a look if you can find them – they were designed to cope with extreme wet weather let alone a little steam from the shower.

Decorative details add some colour in a discreet and gentle way. A vintage 1930s spriggy quilt offers some extra warmth on cold nights in one of our wooden cabins, where a Victorian saucer is used as a soap dish (this page). If you have kids, make sure you get the biggest bed that you can fit in your space so that everyone can climb in! In this simple, tiny bedroom we have used chunky panelling to make the room feel cosy and snug rather than cramped (opposite). The pretty floral prints and accessories add a dash of femininity.

Don't be afraid to introduce some rougher textures into your boudoir, as this can help to create a 'back to nature' feel that is surprisingly conducive to a good night's sleep. This rustic bed, made from green wood, is wildly romantic and softens the hard edges of the corrugated metal walls (left). An old wall panel complete with peeling paper has been used as a bedhead and lends this simple bedroom an air of faded grandeur (opposite left). There is something really appealing about bathrooms that have a pared-back, monastic feel, as these two examples show (opposite above and below right). The soft textures of the plaster walls and gentle hues create a sense of calm and wellbeing.

Sensual textures and soothing colours have a cosseting, cocoon-like quality that will help you to create a secluded hideaway that feels a million miles away from the stresses of everyday life.

Guest bedrooms deserve attention too, and if you get it right they will make your visitors feel right at home. Although they won't need huge wardrobes and chests of drawers, it is nice to offer guests somewhere to put their clothes, however short their visit. This antique hanging shelf offers ample hanging space and storage for a weekend stay (above). Children just love sleeping in this cosy bunk room that feels like a ship's cabin. An old apple-picking ladder cut in half provides access to the top bunks, held in place for safety with nautical rope and cleats (above right and right). If space is at a premium and you have the space, explore the idea of installing a trailer or caravan in the garden and transform it into a spare bedroom. We decked out this vintage 1970s American Airstream to feel as luxurious as possible, complete with double bed and rolltop tub (opposite).

Visual storytelling really comes into its own in the bedroom and bathroom, as the need for escape is greater here than anywhere else in the house. This wooden cabin takes a 'rustic-idyll-meets-feminine-boudoir' theme to the extreme, complete with wood-burning stove, Victorian bedstead, gauzy mosquito net, cast-iron tub and crystal chandelier (this page and opposite).

This four-poster bed makes a bold but pretty statement in the blue-and-white bedroom of this beach house (above). Aqua-painted floorboards lend some colour to this quirky bathroom in an old railway carriage/railroad car (above right). A custom-made skylight has even been created in the shape of a porthole.

Bathroom storage can become a decorative feature as this elegant, panelled bathroom demonstrates (opposite below left). A marble shelf is supported by reclaimed, cast-iron cistern brackets and holds piles of fluffy white towels while an old ladder offers the perfect place to throw your dressing gown while you're taking a dip. The Parisian-style light was fashioned from a couple of vintage storm lanterns and some wooden dowelling. A tiny, secret bathroom has been installed behind the wall of antique shutters that spans the length of this beachside cabin (right). The antique galvanized steel bathtub has an integral seat so that the bathing position is seated rather than lying down.

WORK SPACES

Home office, study, artist's studio, sewing room or whatever you are looking to create, your work space should be a place of practicality, personal expression and inspiration. When it comes to our own creativity, each of us has a very different idea of what is conducive to those three important outcomes, so we suggest you begin by analysing which kind of environment best encourages your productivity. Some of us like to be surrounded by an orderly mess, where reference material is easily at hand and the organized chaos helps our minds to relax and unfold, while others need their desks to be shipshape before they can even contemplate starting work.

Either way, you are going to need a work surface of some sort. If space is in short supply, a small pull-out desk in the corner will suffice, but if you have the room, then go for a large surface that you can really spread out on. Don't think it has to be a specially designed desk – trestles, a kitchen table or even a few planks propped on some vintage fruit crates would all be big and bold enough for the job. Some individuals and certain activities call for something higher, in which case old factory workbenches or laboratory benches would be ideal. A wall or pinboard to stick up pictures, notes or other inspirational material is a must; a piece of board covered in white linen or painted and fitted into an old floorstanding frame would work brilliantly. For something a little more masculine, try tacking together a row of reclaimed floorboards with some cross bars, and fix that to the wall.

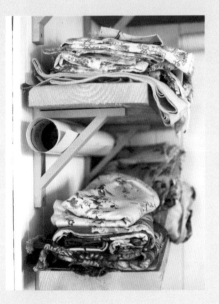

A small flip-down table on piano hinges creates an impromptu desk in an old Airstream trailer that serves as a guest bedroom (opposite). The reeded panelling was especially made and painted to give the interior a vintage feel. We have a passion for fabrics. The problem is where to stow them all. Open shelves store offcuts and small lengths waiting to be transformed into cushions, while scraps are pasted into sketchbooks for future reference (this page).

Striking the balance between inspirational clutter and chaotic mess is a difficult one. Tip the scales too far one way and your creative haven could become overbearing and claustrophobic; too much the other way and you are in danger of it becoming soulless and uninspiring. In this little sewing room, a vintage chest of drawers, baskets and hooks provide plenty of storage for fabrics and sewing equipment, while glass jars full of pins, buttons and threads keep things tidy but not out of sight (above). Our office at Foster House is a constantly evolving space depending on what projects we are working on, with fabrics, furniture and accessories coming and going in all different states of repair or restoration. Working drawings rub alongside more personal visuals created by family members, such as these early 1960s fashion sketches by Gavin Waddell and a watercolour painted by Marjorie Waddell (right, above right and opposite).

ONE-SPACE LIVING

Family life is frenetic, there's no doubt about it, so a home needs to be practical, hardwearing and functional if we are to survive the hustle and bustle of everyday life. Open-plan living suits our multitasking modern lives, because the seamless flow between combined cooking, eating, working and lounging spaces mirrors the way most of us live today. But as the heart of family life, our home is also about much more than just practicalities, and a truly successful one will feed and support its occupants' emotions and moods by creating a nurturing environment that feels safe, cosy, relaxing and stimulating – all this while also looking great!

A tall order, you might think, but not if you remember that the key to ticking all those boxes is to work these demands into your design from the very start, never forgetting that there should always be room for change, since the one thing you can count on in family life is that things will change! Creating zones, therefore, is important, as it will ensure that your home caters for all these needs while giving definition and clarity.

Although it is important to keep a unified decorating scheme throughout an open-plan space, the use of feature walls – cladding an area with natural timber to designate a cosy corner, for example – is a brilliant tool to help define your zones, as are larger statement pieces of furniture, like a huge refectory table or an oversized sofa. If you think you might benefit from closing off an area sometimes, then sliding doors on heavy-duty industrial runners could be a good idea too.

The cream-coloured wood-burning stove provides a warm, focal point in this lofty space (opposite). Decorative elements focus on bold textures and forms so that nothing seems lost or insignificant. The result is an interior that feels light and airy yet warm and welcoming.

A blue-and-white theme carries the visual flow from the dining area through to the cooking area, while the open arch helps to define each zone. The unfitted style of the kitchen creates a laid-back look that helps it blend with the rest of the living space (this page).

Plan the arrangement of your space carefully to guarantee an easy flow of traffic, and always remember the benefits of negative or empty space, which creates 'invisible walls' that will prevent a multitasking interior from looking overcrowded or disorderly.

THE OUTDOORS

Incorporating the outdoors into everyday life is a fast track to keeping it simple, as it feeds our senses and helps to keep us in touch with what's really important in life. Whether it's a small herb garden on your windowsill, a beautiful view, a tiny backyard, acres of farmland or a camping trip, we all need regular doses of the natural world for our health, our children's wellbeing and our sanity.

Food cooked and eaten outside always seems to taste better, perhaps because it brings us back to our roots. It even makes mundane chores such as chopping vegetables and laying the table fun. It also, of course, introduces us to the joys of cooking with fire.

There is something about the ceremony of food cooked on an open flame that makes the meal a real event, and we would encourage anyone to contemplate giving over part of their outside space to an alfresco cooking area, whether it's a barbecue, pizza oven or just a simple camp fire. Portable barbecues and fire pits make great sense if space is tight, but if not, then consider installing an outdoor kitchen, complete with wood-fired oven, grill and even a sink to make the transition outside as seamless as possible. Make sure that you give some attention to your outdoor dining area too, creating a welcoming extension of your home that's effortless to use and encourages you outside as often as possible.

The perfect start to the day: an early morning dip in the sea and a shower on the terrace to rinse off the salt water followed by breakfast in the sunshine. Buckets of ferns and piles of logs surround the galvanized steel tub to provide privacy and to enhance the outdoor bathing experience (opposite).

Simple details are key to enjoying life outside. Antirrhinum, dahlias and *Verbena bonariensis* flourish in the cutting garden (above left). An oil lamp hangs outside one of the cabins (above). Doing our bit for the bee population: our beehive sits out in the meadow where the wild flowers are abundant (left).

Creating some kind of cover or awning will not just keep the rain off or shade you from the sun but also creates a kind of outdoor room that invites you in. Don't stop there, though – make alfresco life as comfortable as possible with squashy sofas and generous chairs, and surely nothing could be more luxurious than soaking in a deep-sided, cast-iron bathtub in the open air, glass of wine in your hand and looking at a beautiful view (left). A small, open-sided summerhouse or simple, rustic structure where you can keep things set up permanently is a good idea and you can then plant the area with fragrant lavender and other herbs and finish with a chandelier or outdoor fairy lights (above left and right). On special occasions it is nice to decamp to a wilder spot at the bottom of the garden (opposite).

Creating an outdoor room is a romantic notion that feels decadent and luxurious. Here, a gazebo has been fashioned out of green wood and rope and draped in gauzy lengths of sheer fabric and saris brought back from India (opposite). The ground has been covered with kilims and a day bed, piled high with cushions, offers somewhere to lounge on a hot summer's day. Instead of a cabin or summerhouse, explore the idea of parking a caravan or trailer in your garden to create a guest room, study or retreat. This 1970s Airstream trailer has been fitted with vintage-style panelling and decorated with floral fabrics and antique linens, and serves as a peaceful retreat or extra guest accommodation when visitors arrive (right).

When the weather is good and we really want to get back to nature, we head down to the bottom of our meadow with the kids for a night's camping. Nothing beats the freedom and simplicity of sleeping out in the open air, although we have to confess that squeezing into a small tent is not really our style and we prefer the comparative luxury of our 1964 Land Yacht Airstream trailer. It's a family affair and everyone mucks in, carrying furniture and equipment down, setting up camp, lighting the storm lanterns, collecting kindling and then building a fire. We often roast a chicken in our vintage aluminium La Cornue camping oven and gobble it down with crusty bread and hot soup (this page and opposite).

Camping out is the ultimate in alfresco living and helps to remind us of what is important in life: good company, wholesome food, simple creature comforts, the warmth of a fire and the natural world around us.